SO-ARY-767

HERE COMES THE APRIL FOOL!

HERE COMES THE APRIL FOOL!

by Charles M. Schulz

An Owl Book
Henry Holt and Company/New York

Henry Holt and Company, Inc.
Publishers since 1866
115 West 18th Street
New York, New York 10011

Henry Holt® is a registered trademark
of Henry Holt and Company, Inc.

Library of Congress Catalog Card Number: 92-53060

ISBN 0-8050-2058-6

Henry Holt books are available for special promotions
and premiums. For details contact: Director, Special Markets.

Originally published in 1980 by Holt, Rinehart and Winston in an
expanded editions as *Here Comes the April Fool!,* and included
strips from 1980.

New Owl Book Edition—1992

Printed in the United States of America
All first editions are printed on acid-free paper.∞

3   5   7   9   10   8   6   4   2

BEEP!

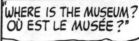

HERE'S THE WORLD WAR I FLYING ACE DOWN BEHIND ENEMY LINES...

I CAN ALWAYS TELL WHEN I'M NEAR THE ENEMY...

GET OUT OF THE WAY, YOU STUPID BEAGLE!

THEY'RE NOT AS POLITE...

HERE'S THE WORLD WAR I FLYING ACE DOWN BEHIND ENEMY LINES WEARING ONE OF HIS FAMOUS DISGUISES

C MINUS ?!!

I WORK ALL NIGHT ON A PAPER, AND ALL I GET IS A "C MINUS"!

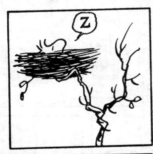

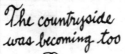

88888's

I'M WRITING A STORY ABOUT THE "EIGHT WHO ATE EIGHTS"

SEE? IT SAYS, "EIGHT ATE EIGHT HUNDRED AND EIGHTY-EIGHT EIGHTS"

WHAT DO YOU THINK?

I 'ATE TO TELL YOU!

NO, MA'AM..I DON'T KNOW THE ANSWER

I WAS JUST SIGNALING FOR A FAIR CATCH!

YOU'RE LUCKY, DO YOU KNOW THAT, BIRD? YOU'RE LUCKY BECAUSE YOU DON'T HAVE TO STUDY MATH!

YOU DON'T HAVE TO KNOW ABOUT RATIONALIZING THE DENOMINATOR AND DUMB THINGS LIKE THAT

YOU'RE REALLY LUCKY

$$\frac{7\sqrt{2}}{\sqrt{6}} \cdot \frac{\sqrt{6}}{\sqrt{6}} = \frac{7\sqrt{2\cdot2\cdot3}}{6} = \frac{7}{3}\sqrt{3}$$

YOU KNOW WHAT I THINK YOU HAVE, SIR? YOU HAVE "MATH ANXIETY"

IF I ASKED YOU HOW MANY WAYS THAT NINE BOOKS COULD BE ARRANGED ON A SHELF, WHAT WOULD BE YOUR FIRST REACTION?

AAUGHH!

SEE? YOU HAVE "MATH ANXIETY"

YOU CAN'T SAY HOW MANY ANGELS CAN STAND ON THE HEAD OF A PIN, SIR... THERE IS NO ANSWER!

WELL, THAT'S JUST GREAT, MARCIE! IF I TRY TO ANSWER A QUESTION, I'M WRONG!

IF I DON'T ANSWER A QUESTION, I'M RIGHT!

THAT'S EDUCATION, SIR!

SORRY ABOUT MY MATH PAPER, MA'AM

ON MY WAY TO SCHOOL THIS MORNING, I SORT OF DROPPED IT IN THE MUD

MAYBE YOU CAN KIND OF BRUSH IT OFF A BIT WITH YOUR SLEEVE.. WANNA TRY IT?

I GUESS NOT

INSCRUTABLE?

NO, MA'AM... I CAN'T SPELL INSCRUTABLE

YOU SAID, IF I TOOK PART IN THE SPELLING BEE, ALL I'D HAVE TO DO IS SPELL WORDS...

YOU DIDN'T SAY I HAD TO SPELL 'EM RIGHT!

I WAS RUNNER-UP IN THE SPELLING BEE! HOW ABOUT THAT?

YOU WEREN'T RUNNER-UP, FRANKLIN...

YOU CAME IN SIXTEENTH...

I WAS RUNNER-UP TO THE KID WHO CAME IN FIFTEENTH!

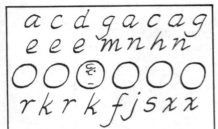

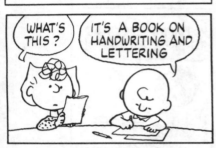

WHAT'S THIS?

IT'S A BOOK ON HANDWRITING AND LETTERING

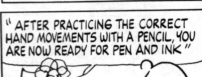

" AFTER PRACTICING THE CORRECT HAND MOVEMENTS WITH A PENCIL, YOU ARE NOW READY FOR PEN AND INK "

" AS AN AID TO SPEED, YOU WILL NOTE THAT SOME LETTERS ARE JOINED OR LINKED TOGETHER "

" DURING PRACTICE, HOWEVER, IT IS BEST NOT TO TRY TO LINK UP CERTAIN LETTERS... "

I THINK YOU LINKED THEM UP!

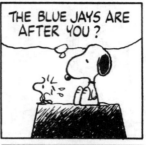

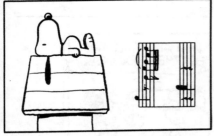

HEY, PITCHER, I'M A REPORTER FOR THE SCHOOL PAPER...

WHAT DO YOU THINK ABOUT WHEN YOU'RE STANDING OUT HERE ON THE MUD PILE?

THE MUD PILE?

I'LL PUT DOWN THAT HE WAS A LONELY LOOKING FIGURE AS HE STOOD THERE ON THE MUD PILE...

THE MUD PILE?

HEY, CATCHER, HOW ABOUT AN INTERVIEW FOR OUR SCHOOL PAPER?

WHAT ABOUT ALL THIS EQUIPMENT YOU WEAR?

DOES IT REALLY PROTECT YOU?

WHAP

OFFHAND, I'D SAY IT DOESN'T

HEY, MANAGER, HOW ARE THE ADVANCE TICKET SALES GOING?

WE SOLD ONE TICKET TO MY GRANDMOTHER

I SUPPOSE YOU'RE GOING TO PUT THAT IN YOUR COLUMN

WHY NOT?

" TICKET SALES ARE WAY UP OVER LAST YEAR "

HEY, YOU STUPID BEAGLE, I'M DOING INTERVIEWS FOR OUR SCHOOL PAPER...

HOW ABOUT A GOOD QUOTE FOR OUR READERS?

BLEAH!

" HE SAID HE EXPECTS TO HAVE ONE OF HIS BEST SEASONS EVER "

"THIS REPORTER HAS NEVER INTERVIEWED A WORSE BASEBALL TEAM"

"THE MANAGER IS INEPT AND THE PLAYERS ARE HOPELESS"

"WE WILL SAY, HOWEVER, THAT THE CATCHER IS KIND OF CUTE, AND THE RIGHT FIELDER, WHO HAS DARK HAIR, IS VERY BEAUTIFUL"

GOOD ARTICLE, HUH ?

POW!

NOW I KNOW WHY WE PLAY BASEBALL IN THE SUMMER...

WHEN YOUR SHOES AND SOCKS GET KNOCKED OFF BY A LINE DRIVE, YOUR FEET DON'T GET COLD!

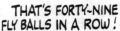

NOW WHAT ARE YOU DOING?

I CAN SEE BETTER HERE

GET OUT THERE IN RIGHT FIELD, AND TRY TO CATCH THE BALL!

AND I DON'T WANT TO HEAR ANY EXCUSES TODAY!

DON'T TRY TO TELL ME THAT THE SUN GOT IN YOUR EYES! OR THE MOON, EITHER! OR THE CLOUDS, OR THE SMOG OR THE CRAB GRASS!

I DON'T WANT TO HEAR ABOUT THE GROUND MOVING, OR YOUR GLOVE BENDING OR YOUR SHOES COMING LOOSE! ALL I WANT TO HEAR IS THAT YOU CAUGHT THE BALL!

PLUNK

ACTUALLY, I WAS KIND OF LOOKING FORWARD TO A NEW EXCUSE...

SCHULZ

WHAT'S THAT YOU'RE WEARING AROUND YOUR NECK, CHARLIE BROWN?

IT'S A MEDICAL TAG...LOTS OF PEOPLE WEAR THEM...

WHAT DOES IT SAY?

"INSECURE"

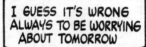

I GUESS IT'S WRONG ALWAYS TO BE WORRYING ABOUT TOMORROW

MAYBE WE SHOULD THINK ONLY ABOUT TODAY...

NO, THAT'S GIVING UP...

I'M STILL HOPING THAT YESTERDAY WILL GET BETTER

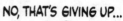

IT'S YOUR TURN.. ROLL THE DICE!

WHAT IF ROLLING THESE DICE LEADS ME TO A LIFE OF GAMBLING?

WHAT IF I CAN'T STOP? WHAT IF I BECOME A COMPULSIVE GAMBLER? WHAT IF I...

ROLLING DICE CAN RUIN YOU...SO CAN **NOT** ROLLING DICE!

THERE...I MOVED FIVE SQUARES..NOW, IT'S YOUR TURN...ROLL THE DICE!

IN THE TWENTY-EIGHTH CHAPTER OF EXODUS, IT TELLS OF 'URIM AND THUMMIM'.. SOME SCHOLARS SAY THESE WERE SMALL STONES LIKE DICE

THESE DICE WERE USED TO OBTAIN THE WILL OF GOD WHEN DECISIONS HAD TO BE MADE, AND...

ROLL THE DICE!

THAT'S A GOOD DECISION

ARE YOU GONNA PLAY THIS GAME OR NOT?

IF YOU ARE, ROLL THE DICE!

YOU'RE SURE THIS ISN'T GAMBLING?

THIS IS A KID'S GAME! ROLL THE DICE!

WHAT IF I COME UP SNAKE EYES?

IF YOU ROLL A SIX, YOU LAND IN THE WITCH'S DUNGEON

IF YOU ROLL A TWELVE, YOU GET TO GO TO "HAPPY PIGGYLAND"

I DON'T THINK I SHOULD ROLL THE DICE... I DON'T WANT TO RISK BECOMING A COMPULSIVE GAMBLER...

DON'T YOU WANT TO GO TO "HAPPY PIGGYLAND"?!

I WANT YOU TO LEARN THE NAMES OF EVERY TREE AND PLANT THAT WE SEE...

I ALSO WANT YOU TO LEARN THEIR LATIN NAMES...GOT IT?

!!!!

STOP SAYING, "HAIL, CAESAR!"

AS WE WALK THROUGH THE WOODS, WE CAN OBSERVE COUNTLESS TINY INSECTS...

WE CAN SEE ANTS, BEETLES, CUTWORMS, THRIPS, MEALYBUGS... ALL SORTS OF CREATURES

!!!?

NO, OLIVIER, I'VE NEVER SEEN A THRIP TRIP...

HEE HEE HEE HEE

A HIKE THROUGH THE WOODS IN THE SPRING CAN BE A JOY AND AN INSPIRATION...

IT CAN REVIVE YOUR SPIRITS, AND IT CAN..

.. GET YOU INTO MORE TROUBLE THAN YOU EVER DREAMED OF IN YOUR WHOLE STUPID LIFE!

FINE BUNCH OF BEAGLE SCOUTS YOU GUYS ARE!

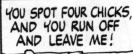

YOU SPOT FOUR CHICKS, AND YOU RUN OFF AND LEAVE ME!

YOU ALL FORGOT YOUR BEAGLE SCOUT OATH, "DON'T CUT OUT ON A FRIEND"

INCIDENTALLY, DID YOU HAVE A GOOD TIME?

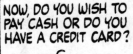

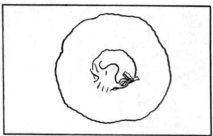

WHAT ARE YOU DOING HERE? YOU'RE SUPPOSED TO BE OUT SOMEWHERE SITTING ON A BRANCH CHIRPING

THAT'S YOUR JOB...PEOPLE EXPECT TO HEAR BIRDS CHIRPING WHEN THEY WAKE UP IN THE MORNING...

CHIRP!

YOU ONLY CHIRPED ONCE... YOU CAN'T BRIGHTEN SOMEONE'S DAY WITH ONE CHIRP!

CHIRP CHIRP CHIRP CHIRP CHIRP CHIRP

THERE, NOW! DIDN'T THAT GIVE YOU A FEELING OF REAL SATISFACTION?

THE BAD NEWS IS YOU'RE SUPPOSED TO DO THAT EVERY MORNING FOR THE REST OF YOUR LIFE!

KLUNK

HOW CAN I DO A REPORT ON HANNIBAL, MARCIE? I'VE NEVER HEARD OF HIM!

RUN DOWN TO THE LIBRARY, SIR, AND LOOK HIM UP IN THE ENCYCLOPEDIA... THAT'S WHAT I DID..

MAYBE IT'LL SNOW TOMORROW, AND ALL THE SCHOOLS WILL BE CLOSED..

GOOD NIGHT, SIR!

This is my report. Here it is.

What follows is my report.

Yes, this is my report.

So far it isn't much, is it?

TRUE OR FALSE? I SAY, TRUE! YES! ABSOLUTELY TRUE!

THIS IS ALSO TRUE! EVERYTHING IS TRUE! NOTHING IS FALSE!

THE WHOLE WORLD IS TRUE! WE'RE ALL TRUE! TRUE! TRUE! TRUE!

YOU WOULDN'T CRUSH AN OPTIMIST WITH A 'D-MINUS,' WOULD YOU, MA'AM?

HOW CAN YOU PIG-OUT ON ALL THAT JUNK FOOD EVERY DAY, SIR?

LIFE IS MORE THAN CARROT STICKS, MARCIE

I'LL BET YOU'VE NEVER EVEN TRIED ONE, SIR

WHAT IS A STOMACH THAT'S EXPECTING A CHOCOLATE BAR GOING TO SAY WHEN IT GETS A CARROT STICK?

EXPLAIN TO IT THAT YOU'RE ALL PART OF THE SAME TEAM, SIR..IT'LL APPRECIATE BEING INVOLVED...

WHERE'S LUCY?

SHE'S LYING IN HER BEAN BAG SULKING

THEN I WON'T BOTHER HER...

I KNOW BETTER THAN TO DISTURB A GOOD SULK

SMART

WHO IS THAT?

THAT'S BLACKJACK SNOOPY, THE WORLD FAMOUS RIVER BOAT GAMBLER...

IS HE FAMOUS BECAUSE HE'S SUCH A GOOD CARD PLAYER?

NO, BECAUSE I HAVE TWO MUSTACHES!

YOU KNOW WHAT SOMEBODY SAID CHARLIE BROWN?

SOMEBODY SAID THAT SPORTS ARE SORT OF A CARICATURE OF LIFE

THAT'S A RELIEF

I WAS AFRAID IT **WAS** LIFE!

YOU BOUGHT A FARM? THAT'S GREAT! I'M PROUD OF YOU

AND YOU BOUGHT A TRACTOR? AND A WHEELBARROW? AND A BIG STICK?

WHAT'S THE BIG STICK FOR?

RUSTLERS

WHAT ARE YOU PLANTING TODAY?

BRUSSELS SPROUTS

IS THIS A GOOD TIME OF YEAR TO PLANT BRUSSELS SPROUTS?

WHO CARES?

BRUSSELS SPROUTS NEVER KNOW WHAT'S GOING ON!

WE GARDENERS ARE ALWAYS READING BOOKS AND PAMPHLETS

HAVE YOU EVER STUDIED CROP ROTATION?

OF COURSE

THAT'S WHERE YOUR TOMATOES DIE ONE YEAR AND YOUR RADISHES DIE THE NEXT YEAR!

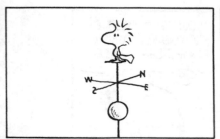

YOU LOOK EXHAUSTED! RUNNING A FARM IS HARD WORK

WELL, OKAY...

I DON'T MIND HELPING OUT ON A FRIEND'S FARM ONCE IN A WHILE...

BUT I HATE BEING THE SCARECROW!

I'VE BEEN THINKING... YOU HAD SUCH GOOD LUCK RAISING AND SELLING YOUR RADISH...

MAYBE YOU SHOULD GO FOR THE BIG MONEY...

YES, THAT'S WHAT YOU SHOULD DO...

TRY TO RAISE A SOYBEAN!

THERE'S SOMEONE HERE FROM THE COUNTY TO SEE YOU...

IT'S ABOUT YOUR GARDEN.. I THINK THE FARMER NEXT DOOR CLAIMS YOU'RE USING PART OF HIS LAND

THAT'S RIDICULOUS!! WHAT DOES THIS GUY FROM THE COUNTY LOOK LIKE ANYWAY?

WHO IN THE WORLD IS THIS GUY?

THIS IS THE COUNTY SURVEYOR..HE'S TRYING TO FIND THE PROPERTY LINE BETWEEN YOUR GARDEN AND THE FARMER...

FARMER? WHAT FARMER?

N 27°

BEEP!

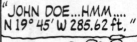

HERE'S THE WORLD FAMOUS SURVEYOR PREPARING A LAND DESCRIPTION...

"RICHARD ROE... N 81° 02' W 184.32 ft. S 61° 47' W 187.15 ft."

"JOHN DOE...HMM.... N 19° 45' W 285.62 ft."

EXCUSE ME.. I THINK YOU'RE STANDING ON MAIN STREET

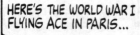

HERE'S THE WORLD WAR I FLYING ACE TAKING A BEAUTIFUL FRENCH LASS OUT TO DINNER...

POTAGE AU CERFEUIL... CANARD A L'ORANGE...

ESCARGOTS...FONDS D'ARTICHAUT... PÂTE DE FOIE GRAS... ET BEIGNETS, S'IL VOUS PLAÎT

UN ROOT BEER, S'IL VOUS PLAÎT

HERE'S THE WORLD WAR I FLYING ACE SAYING GOODBYE TO THE BEAUTIFUL FRENCH LASS BEFORE HE RETURNS TO THE FRONT...

SNIF!

NICE

QUICKLY HE SEARCHES THROUGH HIS PHRASE BOOK FOR THE WORDS THAT WILL EXPRESS WHAT IS IN HIS HEART...

RATS!

HEY, MANAGER, I'M WORKING ON A SPECIAL PROJECT

I'M TRYING TO WRITE AN ARTICLE ABOUT SOME OF THE FUNNY THINGS THAT HAPPEN IN BASEBALL GAMES...

IF YOU CAN THINK OF ANYTHING FUNNY, LET ME KNOW

I DOUBT THAT I'LL COME UP WITH A THING!

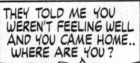

HELLO, SALLY? I JUST CALLED TO FIND OUT HOW YOUR BROTHER IS...

I SUPPOSE YOU THOUGHT I'D THINK YOU WERE CALLING TO ASK ME TO GO TO THE MOVIES!

WELL, I DIDN'T!! AND I WOULDN'T GO TO THE MOVIES WITH YOU NOW EVEN IF YOU ASKED ME, SO THERE!

WELL, HOW IS HE?

HOW IS WHO?

HOSPITAL ZONE QUIET!

EMERGENCY ENTRANCE

GOOD AFTERNOON, MA'AM! I DON'T MEAN TO BE ANY TROUBLE...

BUT I HAVE THE AWFUL FEELING THAT I MAY BE AN EMERGENCY!

I SAW THE SIGN THAT SAYS "EMERGENCY ENTRANCE" SO I CAME IN...

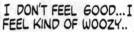

I DON'T FEEL GOOD...I FEEL KIND OF WOOZY..

NO, MY MOM AND DAD ARE AT THE BARBERS' PICNIC SO IT WOULDN'T DO ME ANY GOOD TO GO HOME...

NO, MA'AM..I DIDN'T GET HIT ON THE HEAD WITH A FLY BALL

HEY, SALLY, THIS IS PEPPERMINT PATTY...LET ME TALK TO CHUCK...

I DON'T KNOW WHERE HE IS...SOMEBODY SAID HE GOT SICK AT THE BALL GAME, BUT HE NEVER CAME HOME..

ANYWAY, I'M TOO BUSY TO TALK RIGHT NOW...

I'M MOVING MY THINGS INTO HIS ROOM...

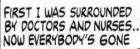

Dear Big Brother, I hope you are feeling better.

Things are fine here at home. I have moved into your room.

Don't worry about your personal things.

The flea market was a success.

I'M SO WORRIED ABOUT POOR CHARLIE BROWN LYING THERE IN THE HOSPITAL...

HE'S GOT TO GET WELL! HE'S GOT TO! OH, BOO HOO HOO HOO! SOB!

IT'S INTERESTING THAT YOU SHOULD CRY OVER HIM WHEN YOU'RE THE ONE WHO ALWAYS TREATED HIM SO MEAN!

AND STOP WIPING YOUR TEARS WITH MY PIANO!

WE CAN'T VISIT CHUCK BECAUSE WE'RE TOO YOUNG? RATS!

JUST FOR THAT WE'LL GO ACROSS THE STREET AND SIT ON A PARK BENCH AND STARE UP AT HIS ROOM!

IT'S A WELL-KNOWN FACT, MARCIE, THAT A PATIENT WILL RECOVER FASTER IF HE KNOWS A FRIEND IS STARING UP AT HIS ROOM...

YOU SHOULD HAVE BEEN A DOCTOR, SIR

THE LIGHT IN CHUCK'S ROOM JUST WENT OUT, MARCIE

HE'S PROBABLY GONE TO SLEEP, SIR

SLEEP WELL, CHUCK!

HOPE YOU FEEL BETTER IN THE MORNING!

WE MISS YOU, CHUCK!

WE LOVE YOU, CHUCK!

WE DO?

WE DO, CHUCK!!

YOUR OWNER'S STILL IN THE HOSPITAL SO I GUESS I HAVE TO FEED YOU

IF I CUT MY FINGER ON THE CAN OPENER, I'M GONNA SUE YOU!

WHO CARES?

A CASE LIKE THAT COULD DRAG ON FOR YEARS

I'M SO WORRIED ABOUT CHARLIE BROWN, I CAN'T EAT OR SLEEP...

WELL, IF YOU GET SICK, TOO, THAT SURE WON'T HELP HIM...

MAYBE IF HE THOUGHT HE WAS MAKING ME SICK, HE'D GET BETTER

MAYBE I COULD SEND HIM A THREATENING LETTER

Dear Big Brother, How are things in the hospital? Things are fine at home.

I have been feeding your stupid dog every night even though he never thanks me.

SMAK!

Well, most of the time he doesn't.

I JUST TALKED WITH CHARLIE BROWN'S MOM.. HE'S NOT ANY BETTER

HE'S NOT ANY BETTER? THAT'S CRAZY! HE'S GOT TO GET BETTER!!

WHAT'S WRONG WITH A WORLD WHERE SOMEONE LIKE CHARLIE BROWN CAN GET SICK, AND THEN NOT GET ANY BETTER?!

I NEED SOMEBODY TO HIT!!

IF YOU SIT ON A PARK BENCH ACROSS FROM THE HOSPITAL AND STARE UP AT HIS WINDOW, THE PATIENT GETS BETTER...

POOR CHUCK..I HATE TO THINK OF HIM LYING UP THERE IN THAT HOSPITAL ROOM

YOU KIND OF LIKE CHUCK, DON'T YOU, SIR?

WELL, I..YOU KNOW... I FEEL SORT OF..YOU KNOW...HE..I...HE..

I LOVE CHUCK! I THINK HE'S REAL NEAT!

REAL NEAT? YOU THINK HE'S REAL NEAT?

I SURE DO! SOMEDAY I HOPE HE'LL ASK ME TO THE SENIOR PROM!

IN FACT, IF HE ASKED ME, I'D EVEN MARRY CHUCK!

COME WITH ME, MARCIE

IS THIS THE EMERGENCY ENTRANCE, MA'AM? WE'RE FRIENDS OF CHARLES BROWN

I HAVE ANOTHER PATIENT FOR YOU.. I THINK SHE'S SICKER THAN HE IS!

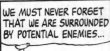

WE MUST NEVER FORGET THAT WE ARE SURROUNDED BY POTENTIAL ENEMIES...

I THINK WE SHOULD PRACTICE SOME DRILLS TO SEE HOW YOU REACT IN AN EMERGENCY...

BE READY, NOW... I'M GOING TO TRY TO CATCH YOU BY SURPRISE...

BEAR!

VERY GOOD! EXCELLENT REACTION!

SNAKE!

GOOD! QUICK MOVE!

BE READY.... BE ALERT...

CHICKEN HAWK!

WELL, THAT LAST ONE MAY NEED A LITTLE WORK..

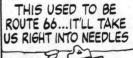

"NEEDLES, CALIFORNIA.. A RECREATIONAL CENTER ON THE COLORADO RIVER"

"ELEVATION, 463 FEET... AVERAGE RAINFALL, FIVE INCHES PER YEAR..."

"ATTRACTIONS IN THE AREA ARE OLD GHOST TOWNS AND TOPOCK SWAMP"

THAT MUST BE WHERE MY BROTHER SPIKE LIVES...TOPOCK SWAMP!

SPIKE! WOOF!

MY BROTHER SPIKE! WOW! IT'S GOOD TO SEE YOU AGAIN!

SO THIS IS WHERE YOU LIVE, HUH? YOU'RE RIGHT, IT LOOKS A LITTLE LIKE MY HOUSE

I'M GLAD OUR MOM NEVER SAW THIS

SPIKE, YOU LOOK TERRIBLE...WHAT'S HAPPENED TO YOU?

MOM AND DAD DIDN'T RAISE YOU TO BE A DESERT RAT...YOU'RE WASTING YOUR LIFE...

IT'S NOT TOO LATE TO MAKE SOMETHING OF YOURSELF... COME HOME WITH ME..I'LL HELP YOU... WHAT DO YOU SAY?

SNIF

WHY DO YOU WANT TO LIVE OUT HERE IN THE DESERT WITH THE SNAKES, AND THE LIZARDS AND THE COYOTES?

COME HOME WITH ME, SPIKE, AND LIVE A NORMAL LIFE...

OH, REALLY? WELL, I CAN UNDERSTAND THAT..

IT'S HARD TO LEAVE WHEN YOUR BOWLING TEAM IS IN FIRST PLACE...

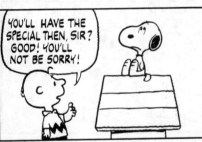

EVERYONE IS COMPLAINING ABOUT THE HEAT, CHARLIE BROWN...

I KNOW...I HAVE TO ADMIT IT'S PRETTY WARM FOR PLAYING BASEBALL

THE ONLY ONE WHO HASN'T COMPLAINED IS LUCY...

SCHULZ

NEXT YEAR I'M GONNA BE A FREE AGENT

YOU ARE, HUH?

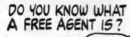

DO YOU KNOW WHAT A FREE AGENT IS?

NOPE

BUT I'M GONNA BE ONE!!

SCHULZ

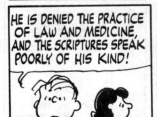

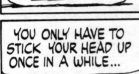

I DON'T GO INTO THAT STORE ANY MORE

I USED TO BUY ALL MY COMIC BOOKS THERE

EVERY TIME I'D BUY A COMIC BOOK, THE MAN WOULD SAY, "GOING TO DO SOME HEAVY READING TONIGHT, EH?"

I DON'T GO INTO THAT STORE ANY MORE

LUDWIG VAN BEAGLE!

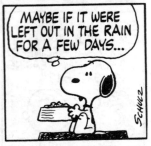